A Voyager's Quirky Journey

Amjadh Ebrahim

BookLeaf
Publishing

Presentation by *BookLeaf Publishing*

Web: www.bookleafpub.com

E-mail: info@bookleafpub.com

ISBN: 978-93-95755-52-8

First edition 2022

ACKNOWLEDGEMENT

I thank God, my family, and my friends who encouraged me to make writing a hobby of mine.

PREFACE

I would store my observations of small incidents and their grand conclusions in my head, only to forget about them the next week. Then, I began writing them down just as notes, but with writing opportunities galore, I can now share them with many others efficiently and see what they have to say about my long-stored and unchecked thoughts. Perhaps, some are interesting, quirky, profound, or dull -- regardless, people's inputs are what inform me, and anyone else, of society's take on the world it lives in and the people it is composed of.

Boxes would have saved the cat

I opened the door and lo and behold,
A flood of matter covering every space.
Like a pirate finding himself in a sea of gold,
I waded through with wonder and praise.

My hand, a student of my eye,
Clutching everything my sight fell upon,
Then putting them back with a sigh,
Headed to where my eyes were next drawn.

Then the lights turned off, turning me blind,
I headed to the door and glanced back in the
dark,
But like a college student, with their young days
behind,
I resigned to fate knowing no point in looking
back.

I returned the next day with glinting orbs,
As they surveyed to make light of this mess.
Ancient star-gazers saw legends around the
globe,
Who shielded them from despair and dread.

I noticed spruce, maple, beech, and willow,

So I put them in a box and sealed it tight.
Black, white, brown, and yellow,
They stayed out of each other's sight.

I came in each day ready to box,
And I became a merry sprite at night,
Gliding by like a stream between rocks,
Among stacks that dwarfed me in height.

Alas the room was full of stacks,
Each box like the one above and beneath,
Each stack with their own name and facts,
All arranged in order like a handsome row of
teeth.

I came in each day not seeing a mess,
Finding everything placed and sorted.
I knew where everything was more or less,
Nothing had to be newly reported.

My dull, dark eyes saw no difference,
Whether the room was in light or darkness,
So I went to the door with no hindrance,
Since they were all one and the same, box and
blackness.

Tale of a Knight

A knight was honoured by the king,
Taking down two cavaliers and three on foot,
But the sky rumbled and the coursing light
caused fire and soot,
So the dazed knight fled from everything.

Everyone left the ground, faces pale, hairs white,
But alas sky's trumpets stopped sounding,
And the ones below were heard resounding,
While everyone returned except for the knight.

He rode to the oracle and asked her,
"How do I end the tyranny of Fear?",
The seer warned, but the knight shut his ear,
So he was told to wait a day for an answer.

The golden orb climbed from ground and sea,
And the knight saw a grey figure by the door,
He opened it and shrieked and fell to the floor,
He raised his head to the spirit and turned to
flee.

But he heard a voice ladylike and sweet,
He gasped and looked up, his eyes wide,
The sweet music flowed from outside,

Where the dread spirit hovered to greet.

The spirit chanted that she was his guide,
So the knight rose and put on his honourary
rings,
And whistled to his horse and brought his things,
So the spirit glided off with the knight behind.

Hours they walked before they reached a river,
Raging east to west, while north they faced,
Then the knight's cocky face was effaced,
As the guide made him tremble and shiver.

She said to enter the stream by horse,
The knight, his eyes closed, shook his head,
The carrion here were waiting to be fed,
Now they shall have their long-awaited course.

But as the spirit beckoned him to look at her,
The knight beheld a light and smile,
That sent him razor-like pins and needles in a
file,
That made the night wrapping her a purple blur.

He grabbed the harness and climbed up,
He spurred but the horse remained still,
"Even he is afraid to empty his fill",
But he looked at her again and whipped its
rump.

Both slave and master plunged into the abyss,
The end, this could be what she meant,
That no living soul can have their fears rent,
Fear is life's contract that no one can dismiss.

But alas! the horse bolted in place,
The knight jumped with a jolt,
And the spirit beckoned them forth,
They waded across at a quick pace.

They reached the other side,
The knight's heart knocked hard in his chest,
He motioned for her hand to kiss and bless,
But checked himself, a ghost. He sighed.

But he saw no green or blue through her,
Only a silver lady not floating but walking,
He reached again and felt fingers interlocking,
Cold and smooth, like ice in winter.

His cheeks burned red as he stared at the grass,
Never had he shamed himself as a man,
Always inspiring awe and fear in his clan,
But just moments ago, he trembled like a guilty
lass.

Hours passed, he told his life story and
distresses,
For he did not see her as his lower,

And she listened, neither absent nor sour,
But smiled and teared, as if it was her joy and
stresses.

From time to time, she would add, "Almost
there",
And he would nod and keep going,
Then they saw the yellow crescent rippling,
So they headed to the mound for rest to spare.

By the moonlight she was silver no more,
But cream with rosy cheeks,
He reached for them and freaked,
Smooth and supple but warm for sure.

She turned to him and said she felt cold,
So he covered her with his bear fur,
She said she still felt the wind stir,
So he pressed his arms around her in a squeezing
hold.

And a statue they remained for a time unheeded,
Until he heard her softly breathe in and out,
So he laid her across the mound, spread out,
And he put the fur over her and receded.

He sat and faced the other way, towards the sea,
And wondered about the oracle's answer,
Whether he will run in storm and thunder,

Not cowering in shame, but retreating bold and
free.

Grey clouds began to form and gather,
Icy and sharp wind nipping at his hide,
But hot lifeful arms wrapped around his side,
And a burning cheek pressed against his, cold
rather.

The knight asked if the oracle will tell him,
Whether he will be free from worry and fear,
Like soldiers in battle with shield and spear,
Standing strong against an army of passions
grim.

She muttered in his ear, "Why does it matter?,
We will give each other shield and sun,
Sailing through this existence as one,
Away or boldly through storm and disaster."

The black bumpy sky growled in stress,
Tears plummeting not from sadness but from
rage,
Heavens' messengers stampeding in outrage,
Flashes of hot white anger glimpsed in the dark
mess.

The lady was embracing him no less,
"Do you still want to know?",

Then in an instant, light struck a crow,
And the knight, costumed with calm, repeated
thrice yes.

Then he felt a hot rain drop and arms released,
A moment later, he saw her some feet away,
"Trade me for boundless courage, you say",
Vanishing, she carried a visage strained and
creased.

The bear rug dropped to the ground,
And slapped the rock-like snow,
The knight was wrapped tight as by dough,
In this rug full of her scent and sound.

The knight knew that this was a trick,
He packed his bags but forgot his horse,
And wandered by a strange course,
Ridden with needles and thorns that prick.

Sky's vein flashed and struck ahead,
Blue-tipped fire raged and compassed east to
west,
The bloodied fool saw no end, so to the flames
he pressed,
A circus freak in a flame dress ran to his next
set.

The clouds' tears blunted the fire's razor heat,

And the bruised and crisped fool did not halt,
"Her good cheer and mournful salt,
I will sup on and will rest on as my only seat.

Let tempest, torrent, and tornado eat my spirit,
Her warmth and smile shall be my favorite rum,
Her words of comfort my trumpet and drum,
Then I will no longer be Fear's slave although I
feel it."

And he saw her from afar waving at him,
She was walking down towards the stream,
Afar he felt her warmth, her face looked
wonderfully cream,
So he ran and ran, as the clouds grew more dim.

Sonnet on Cars

A car lane is a stream flowing one way,
Its twin reversed. They split not by wall,
But paint that wind and rain take for prey,
Paint herds steel beasts wild and tame, stout and
tall.

A rainbow train of cars one by one parked,
Loosely spread, like morning schoolboys in line,
But like before great missions embarked,
Face their chief* as if waiting for his sign.

We drive trusting car lanes will not collide,
Why? Since everyone clings on to earth and
blood.
Also no parked cars face to face in sight,
Wholeness, like the rhythmic chewing of cud.

You read and I'm free to drive with toes curled,
O God, if that's all it was, what a world!

* Same direction

Note: I know cars park to the nearest side
because it's easier, but if the nearest side is

packed, I suspect the car is going to turn around to park on the other side to conform to the other parked cars instead of straightaway pulling in to the other side.

Sonnet on value

"If only my son could get admitted."
My mother, as her friends proudly boasted,
So I paced around the room, brows knitted,
Praying to God before grades were posted.

I got in. Yet, only a girl in mind,
Ghost I was, as I wandered and drifted,
My nose unpricked by Starbucks coffee grind,
Is she mad? No, her heart has been thrifted.

In the hot tub truly alive I felt,
Lapped in burning comfort, ear and nose
pricked,
To each tap and splash fellow swimmers dealt,
Embracing light as it engulfed a mind tricked.

I served people, who would trade bronze for
gold,
In front of God Whose love cannot be sold.

Guilt

Guilt, hov'ring, buzzing,
Draining sweet lustre of life,
Stinging unassumed.

Ode to Bakugan

If I had to recall my childhood,
Like ships in a fog, which can't be erased,
And only with strained pupils to make out,
Their silhouettes drifting away from reach,
I would scramble for images unclear,
But for a memory that shone out through the
veil,
A lighthouse to which if I sailed and docked,
I would be cast on a steel web of thoughts,
And that is the memory of a show,
That I would wake up early morning for,
That I begged my parents and whined over,
That I counted pennies and rolled them for,
To buy a toy from it worth ten dollars,
A show about freakish beasts in battle,
About alliances and rivalries,
About the main hero's rise to the top,
And his journey to the masked archvillain,
Was this what made me buy its merchandise?
And think about it even now with sighs?
I do not know, but perhaps it was that,
But I liked it for something else as well,
Each dueller belonged to an element,
They were Fire, Water, Wind, Earth, Light,
Darkness,

Fire lighted Darkness but hissed at Water,
Earth smothered Wind but was shot through by
Light,
Darkness dimmed Light and Wind whiplashed
Water,
So each element glided and hobbled,
None reigned over all and none proved a waste,
Every one of them boasted followers,
Not one of them shamed with an empty shrine,
Unraveling this spool of memory,
I found along the thread that I liked that,
That all had cause to be proud and shameful,
But this thread is still used to knit my thoughts,
To this day I can't conceive perfection,
Nor can I see flesh and bones clothe garbage,
A genius keeps their room strewn with clothes,
A 'people's' person draws from shoals of
thought,
Some quiet minds are libraries of knowledge,
A kind man can be a tyrant at home,
Rudeness means razor-sharp opinioned minds,
And lovebirds' bond is doomed to fall apart,
Prejudices, but they stem from a source,
A source shining through smokes of memory,
And one rooted deep into my being.

Cinquain on my mom

Mother
Selfless, Sensitive
Cooking, Cleaning, Chatting
Cares for me most
Her departure would break gravity.

Sonnet on friendship

My mother told me to make some new friends,
What, to be a pest in their monastery?
Crawling on the monk's arm, smooth, unhairy,
With his swatting hands cuffed till prayer ends,
And his eager legs bound in criss-cross pose,
"Oh curse this pest! I'm busy with prayer,
A thing more worthless than a strand of hair,
That just strayed my mind by tickling my nose!"

Yet I did talk to a girl after class,
We walked together, chatting, every week!
She even asked to meet in holidays,
We met then and watched a show for timepass,
But then... she asked to meet week after week,
And then I felt like swatting her away.

Distorted Truth

I dig away at mines of Memories,
Ocean bowls and mountains of sand forming,
And childhood haze clearing in the breeze,
No diamond buried, some gold dispersing.

I kick sand and throw the pickaxe away,
And it flips in the air and stabs the earth,
Its handle blinding me in the sun's ray,
I clap my forehead, clap my hands in mirth.

I forgot that it is made of diamonds!
Crafted in the caverns of Media*,
Smelt with the tales of selfless, caring friends,
Hammered with adventure, euphoria.

Yet cooled down with the ice of betrayal,
And smoked with cool, dispassionate murder,
A blade fit for diamonds of its scale,
Not to scrape pale sands for gold and silver.

I leave the axe drowning in the sandsea,
Yes, I cannot fly a broom night or day,
I do not think my friends would die for me,
But aren't we ourselves made of plain clay?

Clay that shrivels without bread and water,

That can burn and numb in the heat and cold,
That fouls and stinks without bath and shower,
And that stings from bees and bugs young and old.

Beetles and centipedes feast on our flesh,
And not a crow stirs to keep them away,
Plagues germinate, grass is still green and fresh,
Millions of graves, and Earth moves without sway.

Foolish to think the world bows at our feet,
To equate our clay selves to Roman gods,
We ourselves are worthless enough to eat,
We are needful beasts, not earth-shaking gods.

So I claw and scrape with bare hand and nail,
And how bright silver dust looks on my hand!
So even strangers' smiles grow unstale,
Thus once desert, now a palace on sand.

 * Media refers to all works aimed for the public (e.g.
works of fiction)

Note: Solid friendships, betrayals, and murders
happen in real-life, but most relationships are
relatively boring and eventless compared to what we
see in fictional cases.

Ego and Knowledge

Brown-rimmed black eyes glued to the screen or
cipher,
And a sprawled hand on a mouse twice its size,
Tick, tick, echoes, filt'ring to a whisper,
Through the night, the screen his one friend and
prize.

"A magician", his peers would praise and nod,
As they glanced at red hundreds on his test,
Stroking their beards covering necks broad,
And his sparkling eyes smiled and he shooed in
jest.

The screen lost its charm and his eyes broke
free,
Now as a sage as everyone claimed,
He thought he knew all things in land and sea,
So the world turned dull and firmly framed.

The screen held dust, his world did no more
grow,
His mind as well, what was there left to know?

Ignorance

It's free, unbounded,
A child may think they know all,
Thus it's restricting.

Transition

A symphony of surging wind and water,
Bearing and guiding sleeping ships across,
On a straight determined course set by nature,
Through stormy discord, shielded them from
loss.

But soon the wind and current slowed and died,
A graveyard drifting for eternity,
Some ships revived and left, being their own
guide,
While some stayed till storm and calamity.

Those that soon left anchored from rock to rock,
Braving the sweeping tides and shaking earth,
While the rest capsized or drowned as a flock,
Some rebounded and strove to prove their worth.

Some docked at the coast on the quiet sand,
But the dead waited. Storms gave them a hand.

Wider World

Chapter 1

My home, a cage that I roamed around in,
Beyond which I was cattle being herded,
Only thinkable way, my parents' way.

Chapter 2

One night, we walked home with friends from
the store,
Parents busy talking, I ran in front,
My arms spread out, embracing the cool air.

Chained, yet I still felt like an explorer,
Wandering in a wider, deeper, world,
Surveying all around me, not just ahead.

Chapter 3

In grade eight, I, my friend, walked to the pool,
Adventurers navigating chaos,
Wide-eyed, striding towards a goal through
mess.

No one to herd me to a stubborn goal,

Where my world was just the path to get there,
This time I adventured in the wider world.

Chapter 4

Now I walk almost anywhere I want,
I take the bus each day to my college,
I can even drive around by myself.

But sometimes I would run in the cool night,
Searching for that sense of awe, adventure,
And missing what I had as a child.

Unhorned Devil

A canine, its torso seemed draped in stripes,
But I reached closer. No, its bulged-out ribs,
Like the pale white hands of the grim reaper,
Grasping the dog's sides, waiting to squeeze,
Its backbone, a mountain ridge hiked by mites,
Shoulders, jutting rocks beneath stretched
rubber,
All were supported on baton-like limbs.

I patted its back, but it turned its face,
Growled at me with its yellowed dripping fangs,
Oil-thick saliva pattering on the tongue,
Which in the heat and stench was a hell-bed,
But even that laid in a deathly frost,
Which was white and pale like a dread spirit,
It seemed its life was poured into its eyes,
Lustrous black mirrors I could not see through,
On them a demon with a frenzied smile.

And the filthy dog stared with a meanness,
My priests, doctors looked at me the same way,
When I entered their room behind elites,
With their fat gold Chopards and Swiss silk
suits,
They shooed me away like I was a rat,

And now this dirty bloody filth-eater,
Which, not who, can't even scare bugs away,
Which shamelessly scrounge on what they can
get,
Cheap, course flesh, wrapped in a tattered cover,
Can you blame the skin? Not wrapping a gift,
But a pile of bones and shriveled organs,
Organs like dried dates in burning summer,
And this abomination dares to bark,
To bare crooked urine-stained teeth at me,
To look as if I'm begging on my knees,
In front of noblemen and their table,
Decked with gold plates of saffron, caviar,
Mountains of kobe beef and Maine lobsters,
I kicked the bitch's ribs, and I heard a wheeze,
Brown islands in the black sea fragmented,
Into countless pieces, once armies of mites,
Till its fur turned light brown except its tail,
So I kneed it, coat leaking to concrete,
I heard a crack, I flipped the dog over,
Its ribcage like the frill of a lizard,
Yet under stretched skin, a bone split in two,
The pieces' ends like edges of glass shards,
Or like canine teeth in an open mouth,
And I heard the dog wheeze again and whine,
A toned down howl, but no friends to hear it,
Or maybe a beg for pity, mercy,
I was not sure, so I wound my leg up,
Stared at the devil in those black mirrors,

Grey oil leaking down from his* mouth's
corners,
Grin showing all his crooked yellowed teeth,
Liquid black eyes staring with a meanness,
And released, the wretch left the ground to fly,
Far from this hell, but it was forced back down,
As if it had violated its place,
That for it, hopes of escape were sins.

It must starve and rot just for existing,
Forever in this fire and soot called earth,
Dwelled, stained by many an unhorned devil,
Who are shackled by the laws of the land,
And who try to climb the ladder to godhood,
Donning smiles and laughs distant to the eye,
Selling fiber garments called compliments,
Most of them loose, sagging on the buyer,
Who occupies rungs above the seller,
Who returns him with an acquaintanceship,
Igniting a firecracker of new "friends",
Who hover over him in the ladder,
But him then clinching on to the nearest ones,
And vaulting up, meeting them eye-to-eye,
Thus going up and up till he reaches death,
In this process he meets a great many,
Who speak with him with a grave, burdened
face,
Who stare at him, like some stare at a bear,
To ward it off their site, to the forest,

Such a world dog and devil were chained to.

But, I still felt a sweet itch here and there,
Like of a breakup after two sweet months,
I cooled my hot brain with thoughts of future,
Of climbing up past those who will regret,
The itch wore off, but for a mere moment,
Before rushing, sometimes flooding, back in,
And at one such time, I saw this low dog,
Which in its huddle of bone, bug, and skin,
I forgot that itch and even my eyes smiled,
Before it** unrightfully left its place,
Then a tsunami struck, with relief since,
I beheld the dog panting in my arms,
I felt for the chest. Its skin was not tight,
It sagged, the round bony vessel of life,
Once standing tall, crumbled into rubble,
They floated to its back like through space,
I heard soft rattles through the rubber skin,
I spread the body out like I would with rugs,
The dog's eyes were still open. I saw the devil,
Who grinned back at me, and now I knew why,
No one came to stop him when he played God.
***

*The devil

**The dog

***Meaning that he could invoke retribution to someone who pricked his pride. I believe God would never enjoy punishing people; I'm talking about the act alone.

Self-deception

Dulls and numbs the sting,
But a buzzing in your ear,
Ears unpricked to horns.

I went on a cruise

I went aboard a cruise ship for the first time,
Towering o'er the sea ten stories high,
The tame beast woken untimely by horns,
Which blared thrice, and only then did it move,
Sleepy, drifting, but with a blurry goal,
Guided to it by its puny master,
Who steered this mountain with only a wheel,
A wheel that determined the journey's fate,
For the passengers but also the beast,
Whether it would be dissected again,
So the beast obeyed the wheel in silence,
But heaving out a long heavy grey sigh,
Bellowing like humpbacks as it trudged through,
Until it reached its long awaited rest,
Where then it entered a heavy slumber,
To languish in the void, in nothingness,
Before horns blared and tore away its peace,
And the beast set off to slog through its life,
Forever bound to this endless cycle.

Star and sea

I'm on a boat, gazing at shimmering stars,
As I throw stones, flecks of milk white
wobbling,
Arcs warping them with their touch, like black
holes,
Stretched like a rubber band along the wave,
But, the echo moves past the breaking point,
And so they snap back into drops of milk,
While butter-like echo slides and melts,
Dissolving into the boundless ocean,
Which it once charged through, disturbing the
peace,
Yet raging coursers rampage the vast blue,
Striking blows that send mountain waves
crashing,
Raiding and harassing sea villagers,
Deforming them while they try to kidnap,
But, they surge past, each moment losing hope,
To realize they trail not even with stardust,
But, retreat to the all-consuming sea,
Vanishing from earth's face without a trace,
The sea leaving no crumb or stain behind,
After which is reigning silence and stars.

Depression

Outside is plastic,
Mind and thoughts your only world,
You fear Past's shadows.